G000122746

WHITE PINE
SUCKER
RIVER

Poems 1970-1990
by ROBERT ALEXANDER

19   NEW RIVERS PRESS   93

Copyright © 1993 by Robert Alexander
Library of Congress Catalog Card Number 91-61261
ISBN 0-89823-136-1
All Rights Reserved
Edited by C. W. Truesdale
Editorial Assistance by Paul J. Hintz
Book design and artwork by Gaylord Schanilec
Typesetting by Peregrine Publications

The publication of *White Pine Sucker River* has been made possible by generous grants from the First Bank System Foundation, Liberty State Bank, the National Endowment for the Arts (with funds appropriated by the Congress of the United States), the Star Tribune/Cowles Media Company, the Tennant Company Foundation, the United Arts Fund, and the contributing members of New Rivers Press.

New Rivers Press books are distributed by:

The Talman Company   Bookslinger
131 Spring Street, Suite 201 E-N   2402 University Avenue West
New York NY 10012   Saint Paul MN 55114

White Pine Sucker River has been manufactured in the United States of America for New Rivers Press, 420 N. 5th Street/Suite 910, Minneapolis, MN 55401 in a first edition of 1,000 copies.

For there is a scent to everything,
even the snow, if you can only detect it —
no two places, hardly any two hours, anywhere,
exactly alike. How different the odor of noon
from midnight, or winter from summer,
or a windy spell from a dry one.

— Walt Whitman, from Specimen Days

Some of these poems appeared in the following publications: *Provincetown Poets, Fat Angel, Cream City Review, South of the North Woods,* and the *Survival Graphics Calendar.*

"The Dodge & That Winter Morning" was published as a chapbook. Copyright © 1979 by Robert Alexander.

"Every Night He'd See Her" was published as a postcard. Copyright © 1981 by Robert Alexander.

"Every Day Martha Thought" was published as a limited-edition series of two silkscreen prints, in collaboration with Dorla Mayer. Copyright © 1980 by Survival Graphics.

"Rain," in a slightly different form, was published as a limited-edition silkscreen print, in collaboration with Mike Tincher (funded in part by a grant from the Wisconsin Arts Board). Copyright © 1986 by Survival Graphics.

I.   AT THE PARTY

3   Where Ralph Lived
4   At the Party
5   Ralph in the Afternoon
6   Ralph Remembers
7   From Where He Sat
10   Bathtub
11   White Pine Sucker River
13   Weekend

II.   FINDING TOKEN CREEK

17   Mickey
19   Somewhere in Kansas or Nebraska
20   Library
26   Was It Louis Aragon
28   A Joe Pass Guitar Solo
30   One of the Guys
31   Every Night He'd See Her
32   Finding Token Creek

III. FOR YEARS MY FATHER

37   My Father Had a Small Lab
39   For Years My Father
40   A View of the Trees
41   Every Day Martha Thought
43   At Night the Street
44   Day of the Toads
45   The Michigan Forest Preservation Co.
48   Rain

IV. CORN

57 Ralph Finds a New Park
58 Corn
59 Supermarkets
60 I Imagine the Fog
61 The Blue Dome & Wispy Clouds
62 The Dodge & That Winter Morning
65 You Might Think
66 In Midsummer There Was

V. GOOD HARBOR

69 As the Plane Left New York
71 At this Moment Perhaps
72 You Come in the Room
73 These May Well Be
75 Vacation
77 Garage
78 Good Harbor
82 Snow at Ten O'Clock

AT THE PARTY

WHERE RALPH LIVED

THE upstairs of my house is a remodeled attic. Perhaps forty years ago they plastered the slanted ceiling and painted the walls a dull green, perhaps it was a bright green at the time but it's faded over the years and now it's a dull light green. The floors are painted brown. The walls on the third floor of the house I grew up in were painted the same green, but what's even more remarkable is that my attic these days smells the same as that other attic, no doubt it's the smell of old plaster. It makes me think of rainy afternoons with the electric trains whizzing back and forth across the dull green room.

These early spring mornings I often walk the dog the few blocks down to pick up the newspaper, then home along the Chicago and Northwestern tracks. It's often cloudy, in April, and the wind is still cold and my dog, a border collie whose ten years have only slightly moderated her energy, runs up and back across the backyards. We walk home by the Theo. Kupfer Iron Works, the Morris Heifetz Salvage truck out back with its hand-painted motto "Scrap is Forever." Down the tracks, beyond a gravel loading yard the Garver's Supply Co. warehouse is like a Charles Sheeler painting, all light and surfaces, the faded white words, the gray superstructure of the grain elevator rising toward the clouds.

AT THE PARTY

RALPH has just bought himself a new pair of red sneakers. The catalpa tree beyond his porch has fragrant trumpet-shaped flowers among the huge leaves. When Ralph looks closely at the catalpa flowers he sees on the pale blooms red streaks the same color as his new sneakers.

Across the street spring pigeons call each other names. She sat there, the window was open and the surf of traffic mixed with the warm air.

Saturday night, at the party, Fred asks him, Why red? They were on sale, says Ralph, the only ones left. When Ralph gets home the night air is still warm and, falling asleep, he can smell the catalpa flowers.

RALPH IN THE AFTERNOON

RALPH goes to the park. It's late summer, one of the last warm days, well after Labor Day so the park is empty. Some of the trees are beginning to turn yellow and red. The wind is from the southwest, blowing warm across the lake. Ralph's dog runs into the waves and waits for Ralph to throw the frisbee. But it's too windy, the frisbee won't go against the wind, falls into the waves.

Out in the waves Ralph sees what looks like a large stick, sinking and resurfacing, but when he looks again he sees the head and neck of a turtle. Last spring out on the grass he had seen a turtle at least a foot across about to lay eggs perhaps, surprised by the young boys coming closer. Ralph picked it up and took it over to the water. It's amazing how fast they move when you let them go, he thought as he put it down and it scooted into the waves. It seems to Ralph throughout the summer that every day, around two-thirty in the afternoon, when he brings his dog to the park to go swimming, he sees the dark head moving against the shiny water. Always in the same direction (but never as close, never as clear, as today). The turtle's head disappears quickly when Ralph's dog goes crashing into the water.

Ralph and his dog walk up by the creek; the cattails are still green, brown here and there but mostly green. There's a kingfisher that Ralph has seen often, today he's facing into the wind, hanging over the water wings steady . . . and suddenly plunges, wings folded, to catch a fish. Ralph's dog is grazing on the quackgrass that grows close to the water.

RALPH REMEMBERS

RALPH remembers what it was like, as a child, walking up to the Coolidge Corner library. He would walk along the back alley behind the 1200 Beacon St. motor hotel they built a few years back (he used to walk down there with his mother to look at the hole in the ground that seemed at the time impossibly deep, the center of the earth he looked into, water and mud, SLAM SLAM of the pile driver) and breathing the exhaust of the kitchen fans, the smell of grease, he'd walk alone up to Coolidge Corner. The huge plate glass windows of the library faced west, so the librarian pulled amber plastic shades down in the afternoon. In an amber fog Ralph went through section after section of the books, Geography, then History, Biography. When the librarian asked if he needed help he said, Thanks, just looking.

It's Saturday and the wife, as Ralph says sometimes if no one's listening, is off at a conference. Ralph remembers a Christmas vacation when all he did was read Raymond Chandler lying on the couch in front of the wood stove, alone in the house. Ralph remembers the garage sale in the paper, as he steps out of the shower, it's a warm autumn afternoon he'll drive up by the lake blue blue to the east, perhaps he'll find an old photograph taken when the kid was just off the boat. . . . Or, better yet, a new reading lamp for his desk.

FROM WHERE HE SAT

FROM where he sat Ralph could see the top of the University buildings peeking over the crest of his neighbor's elms. They were elms, weren't they? What the hell, he'd been over it in his mind several times and they were definitely elms. . . .

From the next room Martha: Elms, dear? Did you say elms? No question about it, they were elms.

He wrote: "This street is silent. Outside my window a silver maple drops yellow leaves onto weeds and bricks. . . ."

It was Sunday afternoon and in the next room the TV with the football game he'd just turned off. Outside the windows his neighbor's elms were yellow already, leaves streaming in the wind off the lake. Angela had been born in Port Washington, her parents Republicans, realtors, her mother working back in the sixties – and perhaps a church project or two when Angela used to sneak off to Milwaukee and hang out in the Public Museum.

Once a week he would walk up to class and spend a couple of hours looking at Angela's pre-Raphaelite face across the table, the windows growing dark outside the concrete building . . . that Yeats poem, he'd slip it into her mailbox someday.

In the hallway she had touched him once: "I don't date married men, generally speaking." She was writing a paper on Sylvia Beach.

He remembered his father walking the halls of the hospital, tinsel still on the Christmas tree, telling a joke he'd heard first maybe when he'd reached puberty twenty years before. "I don't generally but you talked me into it" after "I'm a man of few words do you or don't you."

In the autumn wind, yellow leaves, a hint of rain . . . and she touched him in the hallway, beyond the windows the skyline and the lake.

Fall and he'd sit on the back porch – or was it the front porch, he'd never really been sure – looking off across the fields at the telephone poles he liked to exercise his eyes by focusing on . . . the gravel of the driveway, year by year, becoming thicker with weeds.

And Angela. Walking beneath the yellow leaves: "We moved to Port Washington when I was fourteen. We used to walk out on the breakwater in the middle of the summer for the cool breeze. My father worked for the power company and at Christmas we always baked almond cookies."

When he'd gotten back to the farm at the end of summer, he'd sit out on the porch in the September darkness. Frank was living out there then and they'd go together to do the laundry down in Sauk City, eat dinner at the Penguin. Now he'd cut his hair and was working for a computer company. "The long evenings out on the river in the canoe, just me and Frank watching the Great Blue Heron."

They went out to visit the place. He remembered the phone call in the night – he thought it was his father at first then remembered his father had died six months before – "The farm burned to the ground last night, no one hurt but I lost everything but my guitar." It was October by then and the trees . . . the oaks russet, the wind through the dead and dying leaves of the cottonwood. There was a big hole in the ground that used to be the basement where he stored the books one summer when he and Martha had gone out west and Frank's waterbed had leaked and he'd lost the first edition of Yeats and the Byron his great-grandmother had carried from Brooklyn to St. Louis. There were trees growing out of his basement.

Now in the October wind the leaves blew and from the next room Martha: Elms, dear, did you say elms? By now it was a joke, the two of them walking along the beach, and barely heard over the roar of the surf "Elms, dear. Did you say elms."

Angela, was that really her name . . . what had Donna said at the party, Are you two going to jump into bed or what. Or what, I guess. "I used to have a first edition of Yeats but the waterbed leaked . . . not mine, but what can you do."

Beyond the window there was the shadow of the porch and beyond the backyard some trees. From where Ralph sat he could see the trees and, beyond them, some concrete. Martha in the next room moving back and forth: The elms, don't forget the elms. "The basement, he could see the basement now naked in the afternoon. Gray clouds over the hill."

BATHTUB

It's getting to the end of winter. There are dusky cardinals gathering around Ralph's bird feeder, just feet from his study window, and he can see them beginning to sprout rust-colored feathers. He likes particularly one who has among dun feathers only a carrot-orange beak, just a spot of color like an enormous red nose.

On cold days the sky is still a glacial blue above the white snow like January at its coldest. There's been a light snowfall through the night and this morning the sun bright as summer. But the buds on the walnut in Ralph's backyard are late bloomers, last year not swelling until April, no leaves until almost the end of May.

Ralph's dog has picked out a spot near the tree to roll in the snow, throughout the winter she's formed a depression in the snow that he's come to think of as her bathtub. In the top of the walnut a bright red cardinal takes a long solo. Squirming on her back Ralph's dog makes angels in the fresh snow.

RALPH takes a walk with his dog. It's late August, an afternoon of bright warm sun, at least away from the Lake where the wind blows straight off the cold waves. Yesterday Ralph watched that wind at work moving the great dunes along, throwing sand back over the spruce all along the top of the cliffs.

Yesterday they went walking down from the dunes, looking out through spruce and mountain ash (still green with bright red berries) at the waves and white foam advancing before the northwest wind. When they come out onto the beach the wind whips sand into their eyes.

Ralph's dog stands, back turned to the wind, watching the cliff: as the wind loosens sand and carries it over the dunes rocks the size of golfballs and baseballs come rolling down, first one, close by, then another, twenty yards off, then another, closer, in the other direction. Ralph's dog, surprised, jumps back as a rock the size of a large orange comes splashing through a pool left by the Lake. And all the while the waves crash and roll the rocks on the beach, grinding them into sand their ancestors have long since become.

But today Ralph and his dog have walked back into the woods. It's quiet here, away from the Lake. And soon Ralph realizes that mostly, along the lake's edge, he's seen red pine and spruce . . . but here they've been walking through a large stand of white pine.

Ralph and his dog soon come to where the Sucker River crosses the trail. The river has cut through the dunes here on the way to the Lake, and Ralph walks up to the lip of the cut, looking down over roots and over-hang down the steep sandy slope to the stream. He swings over the edge and leaps down the sand, enormous strides taking him in seconds to the water. His dog whines and runs along the edge of the cut until she finds a spot slightly less steep and launches herself over the edge and down the shifting sand.

Here at the bottom the water runs over sand and fallen branches. Ralph sits by the stream and raises his face into the sun.

Ralph opens his eyes. Years have fallen away. He sees down the cut an enormous white pine standing just beneath the sun. Its branches hang wide over empty space.

The white pine is huge, centuries old. One day, Ralph thinks, the sand will fall away from the roots just one handful too much and the pine will topple into the Sucker River. But now, with the sun hot on his face, Ralph sits on the grass and sand of the stream's edge. When he looks again Ralph sees way up along the edge of the cut his dog walking back toward him. She's gone a long way down the stream to find a less steep way up the bank. She must be impatient, Ralph thinks. He gets up stiffly and climbs up the bank to follow her.

WEEKEND

ALL weekend long it rained and the wind blew leaves and walnuts out of the tree in Ralph's backyard. There was occasional lightning and Ralph heard the booming of walnuts on the roof as rather benign artillery, though he wouldn't want one to hit him on the head.

On Monday the rain had stopped and Ralph woke to the sound of geese squawking up beneath the still-solid clouds. The walnuts were mostly gone from the tree (for another two years), the leaves also, the bare branches looking already in mid-September like they would in the middle of winter. Walnuts lay across the lawn like small green baseballs . . . over a hundred, Ralph figured, on his small patch of backyard. All day long Ralph looks out his window to see the squirrel so flushed with food he's doing acrobatics on the hammock. He leaps from the tree, runs, stops, jumps up to the hammock, holds on for a few seconds, then flips in the air, once, twice, again . . . and jumps back to the tree.

At dusk, when light is barely light, one of Ralph's cardinals comes to feed at the feeder just beyond his window. Ralph has come to think of the birds as his, he supposes it's the same pair he sees, always this time of year by themselves. In the spring Ralph noticed how, holding a single seed in their breaks, they would give each other sunflower seeds. But now they come alone, and the quiet sounds Ralph hears like squeaks while they peck at the sunflower seeds are, he would like to imagine, for him.

FINDING TOKEN CREEK

MICKEY

FOR a week or two he was having everyone call him Mickey. At first he just said If you'd see the movie you'd understand and pretty soon everyone had seen the movie and he went back to being just Morty. That was winter. We were meeting then a couple of times a week in the morning at the JCC to play racquetball. Mornings were the only time you could get a court, besides it was cheaper too. Morty was working second shift at the hospital, and I had Tuesdays and Thursdays off.

In the shower he would tell me about the drugs he mixed up for the terminal patients. Morty was a pharmacist, the end of a long road from the Bronx and a spell pig farming in Mt. Horeb. Then he got asthma from the pigs, no wonder, what's a nice Jewish kid from the Bronx doing raising pigs for Christ's sake? He'd bring his inhaler with him onto the court. My strategy therefore – he was also a bit overweight, a swimmer who years ago had stopped competing – was to get him running back and forth. I got a kick out of hearing him wheeze. No doubt because, a better player by far, he usually beat the shit out of me.

That winter was no fun anyway. The wind comes off the frozen lake in Milwaukee, from the pool of the JCC you can see through the misted wall of windows – what the hell's it cost to heat that place I wonder – a white expanse of ice snow and cloud. Still sweating in my long underwear I'd walk with Morty in the biting wind to get breakfast at the nearby Mafia hotel. I'd nearly been threatened there in the restaurant once when I complained about the dessert, but I figured they wouldn't recognize me in the coffeeshop. By the time spring came, a month or two later, Morty was thinking about moving to Toronto, and Tuesdays and Thursdays I had started sleeping in.

It snowed often that winter and the bridge to the harbor became an eight-lane mountain of slush, spin up one side and slide down the other, where we saw few other cars but occasionally a swarm of trucks. I thought of putting skis on the car and saving ourselves some time on the way down.

It's the biggest small town in the world, they often say about this city – and it's true, from the other side of the bridge it all seems like the edge of a town somewhere in Kansas or Nebraska, the even flat streets receding up a slight incline to the wheatfields, two-story houses antique glass in the windows flickering at you as you walk down to the corner grocery. What's different here is that the corner grocery stocks kielbasa and other Baltic delicacies.

That year as I studied in my small room the intricacies of Gothic architecture I conceived of the wide span of the bridge – more often than not empty as we crossed it, the lights of the harbor strung out like a small-town square beneath us – as a kind of giant cathedral, Lake Michigan to the east, the sky dark overhead . . . and no traffic on the eight-lane highway. What kind of pork barrel do you suppose this was anyway? you ask one night as we rush freewheeling down to the harbor.

LIBRARY

We might have given birth to a butterfly
With the daily news
Printed in blood on its wings

— Mina Loy

YOU'VE been in the library now for hours. You came back after dinner and now you've fallen asleep. As a matter of fact it's so late that everyone else has left the library, but since you're tucked away in a corner by the window no one noticed you before they turned off the lights. It's April now and the moon is almost full and the clouds are scudding across the moon so it looks like the moon itself is moving quickly . . . and off to the east the lake is dark, though even if you were awake you couldn't see the lake from here, where you're sitting by the window – or more factually, slumped over with your head back and your mouth open as though you'd fallen asleep on a plane. Books, several of them, are open in front of you.

On December 10, 1929, Harry Crosby, 31, and Josephine Rotch Bigelow, 22, were found dead together in a friend's apartment. They'd been lovers for a year and a half, though each was married to someone else. The *New York Times* the next day had this to say:

> The couple had died in what Dr. Charles Morris, Medical Examiner, described as a suicide compact. The police believe that Crosby, in whose hand they found a .25 Belgian auto-

20

matic pistol, had shot Mrs. Bigelow and then turned the weapon on himself. There were no notes and the authorities were unable to obtain information pointing to a motive for the deaths.

In the dark library, in the overstuffed library chair, with the moon asserting itself through the windows your sleep is getting restless. It's almost, with the moon and the dark library, as though you're not asleep at all. It's as though you're hearing voices from far off, as if you're walking in a fog down a city street and there are people talking all around you but you can only see the glow of distant street lights and dark trees formless around you . . . and then suddenly faces appear out of the fog. This has all happened before, as a matter of fact you've been troubled with these dreams for months, but they've never been this vivid. The faces circle you, indistinct in the fog, and for the first time you can hear what they're saying. . . .

Caresse Crosby: The lazy towers of Notre Dame were framed between the curtains of our bedroom windows.

Harry Crosby: "I like my body when it is with your body. It is so quite new a thing."

Stephen Crosby: The idea of your writing poetry as a life work is a joke and makes everybody laugh.

Caresse: There was a swimming pool on the stream side of

the courtyard, around whose paved shores coffee and croissants were served on summer mornings from sunrise until noon.

Harry: The shattered hull of a rowboat stuck in the sand, a fire of driftwood, a bottle of black wine, black beetles, the weird cry of seagulls lost in the fog, the sound of the tide creeping in over the wet sands, the tombstone in the eel-grass behind the dunes.

Hart Crane: Dinners, soirées, poets, erratic millionaires, painters, translations, lobsters, absinthe, music, promenades, oysters, sherry, aspirin, pictures, Sapphic heiresses, editors, books, sailors.

Harry: What is it I want? Who is it I want to sleep with?

Josephine Rotch: Do not be depressed. Take the next boat. You know I love you and want you.

It's hard to believe you're still asleep, slouched over in the musty library chair. The moon is still poking through the clouds. If your eyes were open you'd see moonlight across the books in front of you. But you're still asleep, cramped and uncomfortable as it must be. Perhaps you'll ache tomorrow. Outside the window the trees are dark in the shadow of the library. The faces turned toward you in the fog are indistinct – a crowd of strangers who seem, unaccountably, familiar. Like the time you met her at that party, from across the room and all the noise you thought to yourself Where have

I seen her before? knowing that you probably never had. And in bed the first time together, her dark eyes looking at you: Who is this woman? Yes, in the dark library, in the moonlight and the fog, you can hear the voices . . . what is it they're saying, what is it?

> Archibald MacLeish: My impression was that it was all good fun, good decor, but not to be taken seriously. My own conviction was that he wasn't serious about it, till I found out the hard way that he was deadly serious about it.

> Harry: When I got home a riot with Caresse and she started to jump out the window got halfway over the balcony rail. It happened so quickly that I hardly had time to be frightened but now three hours later I am really frightened I hope I don't dream about it.

> Josephine: I love you I love you I love you.

> Harry: It was madness, like cats in the night which howl, no longer knowing whether they are on earth or in hell or in paradise.

> Josephine: Death is *our* marriage.

> MacLeish: As I sat there looking at his corpse, seating myself where I wouldn't have to see the horrible hole in back of his ear, I kept saying to him: you poor, damned, dumb bastard.

You're awake suddenly in the dark library. The lights from Sonny's across the street are out, it must be after four. The moon is gone. You feel like shit. Time to walk the couple of blocks home in the April darkness . . . and the birds maybe already awake. You open the library door, the air's a bit chilly. There's nothing like the taste of last night's coffee, you mumble to yourself and whoever else might be listening.

NOTES

1. The *New York Times*, December 11, 1929, quoted by Malcolm Lowry, *Exile's Return: A Literary Odyssey of the 1920s* (1934; rev. ed. New York: Viking Press, 1951), p. 282.

2. Caresse Crosby, *The Passionate Years* (New York: The Dial Press, 1953), p. 105.

3. E. E. Cummings, as (mis)quoted by Harry Crosby, *Shadows of the Sun: The Diaries of Harry Crosby*, ed. Edward Germain (Santa Barbara: Black Sparrow Press, 1977), p. 219.

4. Stephen Crosby, letter to his son, quoted by Harry Crosby, *Shadows of the Sun*, p. 58.

5. Caresse Crosby, *The Passionate Years*, p. 244.

6. Harry Crosby, "The End of Europe," *transition*, 16-17 (June, 1929), p. 119; rpt. *Torchbearer* (Paris: Black Sun Press, 1931), p. 26.

7. Hart Crane, postcard to Samuel Loveman, *The Letters of Hart Crane, 1916-1932*, ed. Brom Weber (New York: Hermitage House, 1952), p. 333.

8. Harry Crosby, *Shadows of the Sun*, p. 256.

9. Josephine Rotch, telegram to Harry Crosby, quoted by Geoffrey

Wolff, *Black Sun: The Brief Transit and Violent Eclipse of Harry Crosby* (New York: Random House, 1976), p. 209.

10. Archibald MacLeish, quoted by Geoffrey Wolff, *Black Sun*, p. 312.

11. Harry Crosby, *Shadows of the Sun*, p. 277.

12. Josephine Rotch Bigelow, telegram to Harry Crosby, quoted by Geoffrey Wolff, *Black Sun*, p. 285.

13. Harry Crosby, unpublished notebook, quoted by Geoffrey Wolff, *Black Sun*, p. 283.

14. Josephine Rotch Bigelow, letter to Harry Crosby, quoted by Geoffrey Wolff, *Black Sun*, p. 285.

15. Archibald MacLeish, quoted by Geoffrey Wolff, *Black Sun*, pp. 288-89.

"WAS it Louis Aragon who wrote that poem about how there's a moment at the center of a person's life that should be of the utmost significance, exactly half one's life gone by, but that it passes unnoticed a day like any other, dogs barking in the street, newspapers blowing in the afternoon breeze?"

"I'm sure I wouldn't know, dear," she said, wandering among the rocks at the water's edge. The small waves came up the beach and wet her tennis sneakers but she didn't seem to mind, looking intently in the growing darkness at the stones along the beach.

They'd driven off the highway into this cove of redwoods, not to see the sunset since the sun had already slipped into the fog. They'd stopped because they were tired of driving the old Pinto along the coast highway, brakes nearly gone, pumping them up for each hairpin turn. It was already dark here among the mystical trees – so he still thought of them, having just arrived in California. Nearly a decade ago now he'd first seen her working at the bakery, so struck by the blueness and clarity of her eyes that he'd bought a loaf of bread and run out the door immediately, driven all the way back to the farmhouse in a shivering fit. . . .

He was walking by the creek that split the cove in two. In the darkness her red blouse was a blot on the luminous surface of the Pacific. The water ran over sand and rocks and he heard rather than saw it. She had come up behind him in the dark and was rubbing his shoulders. Her breath was on his neck, warm and regular. "Who was Louis Aragon anyway?" she asked. "That friend of yours in Boston you went to high school with?"

A JOE PASS GUITAR SOLO

I'VE fallen asleep in the afternoon. It's November and the radio is playing a jazz program from the local public radio station. But my father and I are in Fenway Park. It's June and the outfield grass is dark green (darker than the huge green left-field wall) and my father has just bought one of those ten-cent paper bags of peanuts (it must be close to a full pound of peanuts for a dime). We're both eating peanuts. My father's hands – which seem huge to me, the back covered with veins "like a roadmap" as he used to say – are deft as hell with the peanuts: Crack and he tosses them into his mouth, the shells drop through the green slats of the seat.

It's the eighth inning and the Red Sox are behind by five runs. Ted Williams is batting and my father points out to me how perfect his swing is. "Look at that bastard swing," my father says, "level as Nebraska." I don't think my father was ever in Nebraska. "But remember, Rob," he says, "he only hit .400 in his really good years. . . . Even at his best Ted Williams missed the ball six times out of ten."

It's getting to the end of my dream. I'm in that funny place where you're dreaming but you're also aware of the room around you. There's late-afternoon sunlight through the plants in my window and it sounds like Joe Pass on the radio, bass and piano comping in the background. Joe Pass's left hand is going all over the fingerboard of his arch-top Gibson and his right hand is in perfect time. The notes are like tropical birds flying from the small speaker of my radio . . . and suddenly all these bright yellow and blue and orange birds come circling and wheeling into Fenway Park. My father and I look up amazed at the bird-filled June sky.

ONE OF THE GUYS

SAM's one of the guys around the office who's into baseball, you know the type, always going around talking about a trade or someone's injury or ERA. Sam's from Detroit. He grew up with other middle-class kids taking cars apart on weekends and going to Tiger Stadium. There wasn't much else to do because the girls in those days liked the older guys who were already in college. So Sam watched the Tigers and completely restored, piece after piece, the 1931 "Tudor" Model A his grandfather bought for fifty bucks in 1950. When Sam had it finished the three coats of black enamel shone in the fluorescent lights of his father's garage.

Sam's getting fat going through his thirties. We used to play racquetball together but then I discovered religion and Sam started taking care of the kid he and his wife conceived after a Grateful Dead concert. His red hair is, these days, cut pretty short.

So one afternoon at work Sam came up with his Al Kaline idea. There he'd stand, number 6 in his old Tiger uniform, looking not a day over forty-five. He'd be holding up a package of alkaline batteries: "Al-Kaline batteries, hit harder, longer!" Not bad, eh? Sam says over coffee. He batted .297 lifetime, you know . . . and it was only in the last two weeks of his last season that he slipped below .300.

EVERY NIGHT HE'D SEE HER

EVERY night he'd see her on the news – she did the weather. It had been six months now since she'd moved out and she'd gone through the whole range of temperatures, starting with a stretch in the nineties when he got back last summer – the avocado, one of them at least, was already dead by then, dropping all its leaves in the heat, so she told him, having kept his plants watered while he was away. And now the temperature dropped regularly below zero at night, she still did the weather her breasts almost visible – but could she know he was watching, some impossible refraction of the TV screen the photons rushing backward. . . .

He still saw her occasionally, their carts bumping in the grocery aisle, by the frozen food perhaps, their hands touching reaching for the orange juice. He turned away at the last minute, before she saw him, turning again as he remembered he needed coffee. He'd started falling asleep right after he ate dinner and waking up late in the evening, his downstairs neighbors had by then already gone to bed – and only once did he hear them making love, tenuous sounds he heard since he was listening. Now late at night he'd make himself a cup of coffee and listen to an all-news radio station from Chicago. This seemed to loosen him up and he could stay awake for hours waiting for the final scores of West Coast ballgames.

FINDING TOKEN CREEK

Oh, and I have watched you, fish
of heaven, here in Wisconsin. . . .

– James Hazard

BEFORE the Yahara enters Lake Mendota, it widens out
and flows through Cherokee Marsh. The marsh sur-
rounds a fairly wide river there, in some places nearly
a hundred yards from shore to shore. From a canoe on
the water there are of course some houses visible, but
often it appears that you are paddling out in the
wilderness, blue water and sky surrounding you, green
trees and marsh-grass, low hills down where the river
flows into the marsh. Along the shore are reeds and cat-
tails, pickerelweed with its large arrowhead leaves, wild
bergamot.

Yesterday was one of the last true spring days around
here before summer comes along and fills the air with
moisture, the sun too hot at midday to stay out in for
the two or three hours it takes to paddle to the river at
the head of the marsh from the gravel parking lot down
at the end of the dirt road that School Street becomes
if you follow it long enough, way off behind the shed
where the highway department stores its winter plows.
The marsh is protected, no cars allowed for its entire
length – and that's why from out on the water few houses
are visible. The wide buffer of marsh between the river
and subdivisions is nearly impenetrable this late in June

with blackberry patches poison ivy and interwoven willows and oaks.

Yesterday the wind was blowing from the northeast. The wind very rarely blows from the northeast around here, only when there's a strong weather system sitting right over Hudson Bay, turning the air down upon us after it passes over the 35 degree water of Lake Superior three hundred or so miles to the north. This makes it especially a pleasure to be out paddling around – my dog sitting in front of me in the bow – since it means that returning I won't have to fight the prevailing north-westerlies that at 10 or 20 knots can make the return trip something to think about. Nothing of that sort this afternoon, just the prospect of a pleasant tailwind going home, easing me along. The sky clear. Air cool in the hot sun. Smell of sun-hot skin.

In falling the willow blocked what could have been the mouth of a stream, but off to one side, what I'd missed on previous trips, is a small break in the cattails – and through it I can see water. I gather speed and slip through, my dog ahead of me unsure of what I'm doing shrinks back from the cattails coming at her from both sides of the canoe, and then we're out into open water, another flowing stream, nearly invisible from the Yahara. Barely ten feet across but deeper than the Yahara, faster flowing and colder. Willows and cattails to the sides, blue sky overhead.

It has rained heavily in the last couple of days, and

the surface of Token Creek is filled with bits of mud moving downstream. The river here twists in doglegs around which I sweep in my short and maneuverable canoe, keeping to the inside though not so far as to get hung up on the little sandbars that form on the inside of the curves. I cross one such bar, sweeping around into the new stretch of the creek, and upstream I see that a willow has dropped a branch or two onto the water's surface, so that mud and flotsam is piled up against the upstream side. And it's here that my dog and I see something remarkable.

What it looks like is a kind of underwater flower, about ten of them strung out just upstream of the willow branches – ten or so flowers the bright orange color of daylilies. And there's a sound like very small pebbles dropping into water. As we drift closer, slowing against the current (I am careful not to paddle, not even to move), I see that these flowers are in fact the mouths of carp just breaking the surface then moving underwater to swallow. These delicate orange flowers are the mouths of feeding carp, huge fish the color of murky water visible just beneath the surface. My dog is watching all this too, she too sees the large fish with complacent faces opening their orange mouths to the creek's surface. While the wind blows uncommonly from the cloudless northeast.

FOR YEARS MY FATHER

My father had a blood factor named after him – at least in Sweden and until they changed the nomenclature, when it became Factor VII. So to the end of his life my father was glad that people didn't get Alexander's Disease but only a Factor VII deficiency. He told me this one afternoon, we were walking through the park. Rob, he said, did I ever tell you the story about the Swedish Academy? But that's a distortion already, he would never have said a thing like that, never have talked about it unless I'd asked him to: Hey, Pop, did you really have a clotting factor named after you? Why isn't it still called Alexander's Factor?

This was a park he walked through on his way to work, along the Muddy River which forms the border between Brookline and Boston. Fenway Park, close by, is named for this same river or anyway the problems it caused – swamps, mosquitoes – for the first white people in the area. A few times my father brought home turtles that he found along the river bank. I kept the turtles in the backyard, by the compost pile where there was an ample supply of worms.

So in Sweden, for a while, I suppose, doctors would call each other on the phone to discuss problems of Alexander's Factor. Sometimes doctors called my father asking him what to do before the patient bled to death. My father had a small lab in the basement of the hospital, you could look up through the windows to the metal security grate. It was dark in the lab most times when I visited my father at the end of the day.

We'd walk home along the river, and he'd keep his eyes "peeled," as he said, for a turtle to replace the one I'd put back in the river, earlier, on my way over to the hospital.

FOR YEARS MY FATHER

FOR years my father practiced the violin: "What d'ya think, Rob, am I wasting my time sawing away on this hunk of wood?" I would lie on the couch listening to him, New York receding behind the glass panes of the living room. My mother of course had to listen to him play more than I, but she too found it a pleasure, not so much from enjoyment of the sound as from what the sound suggested of the pleasure he was having. Often he said that it was his meditation – trying to play in tune, keep the bow balanced and light – and when he died, at home, he had just finished playing Beethoven's Spring Sonata with his brother Josef. My aunt and uncle had come over for dinner, and after dinner my aunt is talking to my mother – who is keeping rather silent, I think – and my father and my uncle are playing. When they finish the last movement of the Spring Sonata my mother asks my father if he doesn't think it's time to stop, and he smiles and says Yes and dies in the chair where he's sitting, violin and bow still in his hands. Later my uncle tells me that while my father plays, "It's as though he's never been sick."

A VIEW OF THE TREES

I thought a couple of months ago that I might try to write a short story. I thought of weekends when people sell old clothes and furniture, coffeepots and dishes that are left from a set someone's parents got for everyday use. There was a special at Sears, and Sears was just down the block, across the river, a few streets further along the avenue. He was a graduate student, she a dietician at the hospital, between them making enough for the one-room apartment with a view of the trees which stretched, a park, along the river.

These dishes sit on your shelf, and you use them sometimes when you have a friend for dinner. Perhaps this is a person you know from work, someone you have thought, more than one slow afternoon, you might have something in common with. Now with the wine and the food you realize you were mistaken. But for once, this evening, you can barely hear the kid practicing trumpet in the apartment upstairs.

1

MARTHA walked from the bedroom, a small room it had always seemed stuffy, facing north, a couple of plants that hadn't managed to grow more than an inch or two all winter. In the kitchen the afternoon sun covered the avocado, the jades, and the hanging fern whose name she still didn't know, having bought it a few months back at a garage sale, watered it and it came back to life as plants did occasionally – you thought you were only getting a pot and zip one morning there was a new plant in the room.

She had often thought that if she could only put Andrew in a pot, water him carefully, feed him every now and then, her life would be complete. The large kitchen would do just fine: there was a spot near the corner away from the sink, between two windows, where one of those large wooden floor pots you could get at any discount store would cover a flaw in the linoleum (the landlord for the last two years had refused to fix it, though at the end of their first year in the apartment he had told her, his face framed by blond hair: If you stay another year I'll fix the kitchen floor).

Every day Martha thought, at least once, about writing Andrew. Even to her that seemed like a bit of a contradiction – Andrew had been gone for three years, and it's probably safe to say she wouldn't have wanted it any other way – but every day, for a moment or two at dinner, or right before she fell asleep, Martha thought about taking a clean sheet of paper and filling it with long certain lines which would speak to Andrew about the goings-on of the neighborhood, what the kids were up to, who was sleeping where. . . . She had never seen his room, in that city where they talked with awkward vowels, but he'd written her about it, about his buying trips downtown where, so he'd said, you could pick up old furniture cheaply, brass from eastern Europe that hadn't for the last half century been cleaned off for the Sabbath.

Martha was sure of that, looking out over the alfalfa field just beyond the window of her studio – she was sure of the brass and the antique furniture and Andrew, sitting alone in his room which smelled musty and, the window open, of sea air from the harbor – Martha was sure that she wanted to write him.

AT NIGHT THE STREET

AT night the street spins webs on the shadows of our room. These patterns shimmer for a moment and then like the ripples of a pond are gone. At the other edge of the pond turtles sun themselves on a log and the weeds flutter.

When the toaster opens, the slice of baked bread slides across the wire mesh. A slight movement. And that's my feeling too, in the moment when the turtles open their eyes, just before they, as paranoid as the next guy, slip into the water.

Worms are pink in puddles along the sidewalk. From across the street there's an earth-and-leaf smell a lot like the park after rain. And while turtles sink to the bottom of the willow pond, ripples disperse on the room's mouth.

DAY OF THE TOADS

YEARS ago it was an island in the middle of a fresh-water sea. That's why now it has the sandiest soil in the Midwest, the dirt roads becoming clay and mud with each heavy rainfall, even at the end of summer threatening to swallow the car wheels right to the axle. Scattered maples already red, birches getting a bit yellow, spruce and white pine dark and lighter shades of green: looking out from the top of this ridge he could tell it had been an island – looking across what had once, he was sure, been a flowing channel of water cutting the peninsula off from the mainland.

We could call it *Day of the Toads,* she said. In national parks: at first they'd attack motorcycles; maybe only suck the gas tanks, like a melon, throw the rest away when they were done. GIANT TOADS TERRORIZE PARKS. There'd be rumors of gangs of motorcyclists eaten by toads, but you know, that's California. Finally our scientists would realize they were only trying to attract attention. Save the earth from a meteor or something.

The clouds were solid now moving from the north. The toads were all over the woods. He had never seen so many. He had never seen a toad as small as the one he was looking at now, on his knees, ass sticking up in the air, head down just inches above the ground. A baby. Maybe an inch long. Had all the composure and serenity of the adults, though. He remembered meeting one on a trail once and they watched each other in the sunlight for minutes before it hopped off. No fear. You're the cutest toad I've ever seen, he said.

THE MICHIGAN FOREST PRESERVATION CO.

It's August. And my wife's not here now, she's gone into town to do the laundry and the shopping. Last week I did the laundry and the shopping, so this week it's her turn. We used to do the laundry and the shopping together, that was just after we'd started living here. Now it's August and we only have to go to town once every two weeks if we take turns. The town is down in the protection of the hills and the bay, and it gets hot there during the day, the sun is up so long these days the sidewalks soak up the heat.

There's a couple of grocery stores in town, neither very good, and of course Dairy Queen and Burger King and the mill down at the foot of the street: pulpwood, mostly. Two years ago the century-old town hall, copper roof and all, burned to the ground – and now there's a concrete-block structure with SHERIFF in neon letters out front.

This is my week off. I'm all alone out here with the hot-sun smell of pines and sandy soil. Here is the several thousand acres of the Michigan Forest Preservation Co. At least that's what the sign says. It looks like no one's been here for years, let alone worked the place, since the Feds decided that plastic ornaments for Christmas trees burn slower than pine cones and are less explosive. Up until then, judging by the boxes of pine cones I've seen here and there in the buildings, they collected pine cones and sprayed the tops with the "snow" that when I was a kid I bought with my sister at Woolworth's.

There are three buildings here. One is an old barn –

a large cavernous space, mostly empty now, in one corner an antique lathe – a barn onto which the MFPC added: stalls to workbenches, vats for the chemicals; and brought electricity – when it became clear that despite the ads in the newspapers out east this was no climate for farming. (Thousands came from Vermont and New York when the land speculators ran a series of ads: "A temperate climate. I've been here three years from New York State and I'll tell you that already I have two hundred acres of all manner of fruit trees and vines that promise to yield the best wine this side of the Hudson." Most went hungry and moved on.)

There's also the front office, a funny little shack that the sign sits against now, on the ground, the sign that's white paint over dark green, growing indistinct with rust: MICHIGAN FOREST PRESERVATION CO. with an arrow – the arrow has a few paint strokes to indicate feathers down by its tail – pointing toward the top of the woods that are beyond the packed sandy soil around the buildings (packed by the vans they used to bring here for the pine cones, I'm thinking, packed so tightly that nothing except sparse grass will grow here for years.)

Then there's the caretaker's cabin, that's where my wife and I are staying, there's an old wood stove in the center, a dresser with a mirror, and a double bed. We brought our mattress with us at the beginning of the summer, turning off the gravel road onto the long sandy driveway that led up through the pines. . . .

Look, she said, the cabin even has a porch. You can

sit here and write and I can take the dog for long walks and collect pine cones. Once when we were visiting my sister in Denver, there were four of us in my sister's car in downtown traffic when a fire engine went by a block or so away, and the dog stuck her head out the window and started howling. People all up and down the street got a kick out of it, laughing and, some of them, staring like they'd never seen a dog howl at a fire engine before.

RAIN

IT's raining. Looking out from his second-floor window he can see the roofs of the neighborhood garages, the elms at the other side of his neighbor's yard blowing yellow in the October wind. As if flipping through postcards he can see other rains: the northwoods with their fir and spruce, the smell of the northwoods. . . . And it was raining, yes, it was raining for the sixteenth day out of the last twenty, the clouds still blowing off the gray surface of the lake and the tent getting, as tents quickly do, more and more crowded, sand in the sleeping bags, crud all over everything.

In ten minutes he has to leave for the office, just two blocks away . . . but for now, sipping his fourth cup of coffee of the day, he can sit here thinking about the smoke-filled woods. That summer there'd been a fire in the bird refuge and the state was suing the federal government because the fire had spread into the state forest, and every day, unless the wind was blowing off the lake, they could smell the haze. It formed the backdrop on the last little drama of his marriage, he thought to himself. You sure talk a good game, she'd said, one of her last comments before that long silent drive home, the car getting hotter and hotter as they left the northwoods for the wide flat farmlands of the south.

It was raining a moment ago, but now, as if in perfect time for his walk up to the office, it seems to have stopped. Water is dripping off the yellow leaves of the elms and off the birches and spruce of the northwoods. The tent is sagging and there's a smell of smoke in the heavy air. Well I guess I better go make a fire, he says, hunger for a hot meal crawling around in his belly. She is quiet now as if not wanting to make a spuriously nasty comment when there's so much that's substantive that she's only hinted at, though they've been talking all afternoon, rain like distant horses clipclopping on the tent roof. As he leaves the house, walking down the creaking bare steps of the front hallway he realizes it's still drizzling.

∗   ∗   ∗

They had met when he was still living in the old farmhouse twenty miles outside of town – back, as he used to say, in the pit of the seventies. It was a cold winter and the wind blew through the thin walls of his northwesterly facing bedroom. He had bought a new carpet and painted the walls a fresh coat of white – and at times it felt like a very cold hotel room that he'd stumbled into in the midst of confusion over whether or not he'd missed the turn in the darkness and was heading off toward Pittsburgh and not, as he'd desired, toward Oil City. He was still teaching school then and she'd drive out in the darkness to be there when he got home. Sometimes they'd drive down to eat at the Penguin, a river cafe with a bar in back that had instead of the usual mirror a panoramic mural of penguins on ice floes sipping margaritas.

By the time they settled into the cold sheets of his bed – her smooth skin warm against his – it would be hours since the sun had set. In some previous ascetic

year he had got himself a single bed to sleep in, and all
night long they would be forced against the warmth of
the other, until it seemed they turned over in unison
through the dark country night.

*   *   *

It's still raining. From the porch you can look out
across the lake at what used to be the Hemingway farm.
As a matter of fact Ernest himself delivered groceries,
as a kid, to my great-grandfather's family. When he (that
is, my great-grandfather) first came up here, and actually
for quite a few years after, there weren't any roads around
the lake, just a boat from the Foot that, long and ma-
hogany, would bring you around to the silence of the
fir and spruce.

There's a road across the lake and at night you can
see the headlights from quite a way off, the road dips
and rises and the lights fade and reappear. Through
darkness the lake laps against the sand. It was an ice
house which my great-grandfather bought and turned
into a pine-paneled summer cottage. The trees of course
have grown up since then and the lake is higher than
it was, that's a mystery no one's quite figured out. The
beach that was more than ten feet wide when people
used to wear long bathing suits is now no more than
two or three.

And it's still raining. It's rained since we got here, tired
of the wet tent, driving through the night and arguing.

The one time we stopped was crossing Mackinac Bridge, looking out through the lights on the cables to the broad expanse of darkness. Now we sit on the porch and it rains, rain drips from the fir and spruce that my great-grandfather planted and from all the other trees that he didn't. My great-grandfather was born in a small town outside of Cracow and came to Pennsylvania when he was sixteen. Forty years later he bought himself a summer cottage in northern Michigan, and now we sit here, arguing, and it's raining out on my great-grandfather's lake, which, like the clouds, is gray as a trout's belly.

* * *

In this dream I'm on a train, it's during the fifties and I'm with some sort of summer camp. The windows are dirty but through them I can see miles and miles of forest. It's only northern Minnesota but to me it may as well be Siberia. The counselors have it in for me, I'm sure, I've heard them at night cracking anti-semitic jokes.

It's important to get back somewhere but I know that's not where we're headed. That's where she comes into it. Suddenly I'm all the way at the end of the train, in the caboose, only it isn't a caboose it's my old bedroom at the farm and she's in my arms. She's the one in my class I've had fantasies about taking to the two dollar movie at the Oriental Theatre. In my dream it's as though I'm seventeen again and in love for the first time. She's everything I've ever wished for and besides, it's clear, she loves me too and her hands are all over me. Meanwhile I'm aware how important it is to get the caboose onto the siding and I'm trying to explain this to her but all I can think about is how sweet her hands are and then

The train has stopped and we're all out in the appalling silence of the northwoods. They've told us to set the tents up and that's exactly what everyone is doing but not me, I'm looking around at the gloominess of the rainy day, the brooding fir and spruce all around, wondering what happened to her. I'm trying to find her, among all the tents, before I wake up, I know she's around here somewhere. . . .

*   *   *

He would remember it as an autumn of rain. All fall he looked out at the roofs of the East Side and chewed his pencil, before, as he said, really getting down to work. On the shelves of his office the stacks of papers multiplied and the rings his coffee cup made on his desktop were the only sign that every day, raining or not, he would walk the two blocks to work. The air conditioner blew in his face as he sat at his desk. Cold air in the middle of November: it puzzled everyone on his floor of the building.

On the occasional sunny day he would watch the white clouds as they scooted above the roofs and the bare trees, the pale blue sky behind them a sure sign of the colder weather to come. In the middle of all the fir and spruce he had finally let his marriage go, watched it trailing out over the lake like the faint smokelike trace of geese flying southward. At the first sign of yellow leaves she had left for California, had in fact already written him about her new friend who taught massage at Esalen. She was happy to be far from the "deep freeze of the Midwest," though in northern California, she wrote, the winter rains had already set in.

CORN

RALPH FINDS A NEW PARK

It's autumn now, it's getting cold. Ralph takes his one-speed bicycle with knobby balloon tires out for a ride this afternoon, his dog runs along beside him. Ralph rides on the dirt trail across the empty field between Milwaukee Street and the railroad tracks – across the grass still green now beneath the wispy October sky. Ralph thinks he'll follow Starkweather Creek, see where it goes before it flows under the tracks and by Olbrich Gardens out to the blue shine of Lake Monona.

Down at the end of Ivy Street Ralph and his dog find a park he's never seen before. The leaves along the edge of the park are green and gold in the October sun. Ralph's dog goes running out across the park as though chasing a deer or a well-thrown frisbee.

And what Ralph's never realized: he sees Starkweather Creek has two branches, which flow together here at O. B. Sherry Park. The willow just at the junction of the two streams droops low over the water. Yellow leaves drift slowly on the water's surface. Ralph looks up the curving west branch, trees on both sides touch each other over the middle of the creek. It's like being in the woods, Ralph thinks – and perhaps the deer would be drinking just upstream from him, looking back at him, curious, this October afternoon.

CORN

Just down the street — it's a white house that needs painting. When I walked by this morning on the way to work I saw the corn growing in her backyard. That's when I knew for sure. She came by the other day riding her bike, swooping over to my side of the street and "Hi" as she went by, I thought at first she was talking to my neighbor who was in his yard but "Who's that?" he asked me. "She was smiling at you," he said.

Corn in the backyard. That would be enough for most guys, I suppose I'd be over there knocking on the door, "Hey, I really like your corn, you know I used to live in the country and it's great to see that special sheen on the leaves here in town. I like your smile too." That's how it could be: leaning my head a bit to see into her backyard.

SUPERMARKETS

SUPERMARKETS. I like the long clean aisles of super-markets: Safeway, Eagle, Sentry – their names like gods of nutrition. I like the anonymity of supermarkets: I'd drive miles to get to a supermarket where I could be sure of not being recognized. Just last week, as a matter of fact, I saw the ex-wife of a friend who lives in a house where my own ex-wife used to live. We found ourselves at the same time by the frozen food, wisps of fog from the freezer spilling over into the aisle. While she was taking her cans of orange juice I examined the 'contents' on a bag of Japanese vegetables. And then, not quite brushing her arm, I reached past her and took a can of another, slightly cheaper brand.

I IMAGINE THE FOG

I imagine the fog has cleared. In the wind. . . . There's no wind today, only rain, a slow sprinkle over pavement and bog, dwarf pine and dunes that shift across road and pine: gentle slavery, this season.

This street is silent. Outside my window a silver maple drops yellow leaves onto weeds and bricks. And now my neighbor wanders in his yard, cutting one by one each of his bright flowers.

THE BLUE DOME & WISPY CLOUDS

THE blue dome and wispy clouds covered me as I came among the hills into town. It was late afternoon. A steep forest rose shadowlike behind a lake off to the left.

Many hours later I awoke sweating in the second-story back room I had taken for the night. When I went outside the pavement was deserted, damp from the mist. Across the street a neon sign flickered "Eat."

I was the only customer, the waitress was about to close the place; she had shut off the grill but made me a ham sandwich. As I sat chewing she talked of a disabled husband, a twenty-mile drive home at night on foggy roads—because she couldn't find a job, as she said, chambermaiding. When I had finished eating I paid her and walked in the mist back across the empty street. One stoplight flashed red above the center of town.

THE DODGE & THAT WINTER MORNING

*"I cant imagine no tragedy worse than being
burnt-out on strawberry ice cream."*

— William Faulkner

THE white station wagon your grandmother hasn't
driven for at least twenty years is back there on the road,
engine ticking as it cools. You've walked into the woods
and are already out of sight of the road; it's so quiet
you can hear flies in the high branches of the spruce.
A deer trail leads off into the forest. Dead branches,
thick and interlaced, stop five feet above the packed
needles. If you were a deer there would be no problem
walking through this forest. As it is you must stoop, but
fortunately you aren't carrying a pack.

*   *   *

I get to work, it's late, or too early, I'm not sure which.
The lights in the corridors are dim, the hallways empty,
the doors as if nailed shut. But that's none of my busi-
ness, for I have somehow left the manuscript lying on
the kitchen table. Here the ditto machine is master,
turning and turning as if in a dream, well-oiled metal
rolling in its cradle. The machine is solitary in its room,
ready to go. When I have peeled away the necessary
layers the motor starts and the ink runs. Smelling of
the laboratories of my youth the copies pile softly one
upon another, a snowfall of white on purple. For a while

all goes smoothly then suddenly something is wrong, copies begin to stir and fall from the machine – but when I reach for the switch it's no longer there, or it doesn't work, the copies drift deeper all across the small table and I am hammering at the switch or where it used to be. . . .

It's all a blur after that, my dream. But in the morning, my students tell me, there are pieces of paper covered with the faint image of a bearded man.

* * *

Above the bay two men at a sidewalk table discuss politics and the approaching war. Lobsters in the tank behind them claw and scrape in the dim light of the cafe interior. The bay lies glittering before them, sails scattered about, open water spreading to the horizon. Before them on the avenue trolleys slide and well-dressed men and women pass close to the table. The avenue recedes, afternoon, beech leaves glisten.

* * *

Out the window the park separates us from the city. Cement buildings rise through the oaks. Leaves are still green, though the air is cold. The furnace in the basement has, weeks ago, been fired up.

The corridors clear in anticipation of the experiment. Some of the sharpest minds in hundreds of miles have gathered this morning in this room of white paint and aluminum. Several even now are thinking of the ocean and the salt-air with long views of the sea and the sky. Seagulls and terns loop through their thoughts this morning.

Out the window the pavement of the city is hidden by trees.

*　　*　　*

Stone houses and white pine cluster to the dunes, the houses growing, street by street, larger, more glass and ivy, the libraries lit up at night, shelves of books rotting in the dampness. Perhaps I should. . . . But of course, sucker that I am, I have left the house too late again.

Still, somehow your face was familiar, as though on a distant winter morning, from behind a kitchen windowpane I caught sight of you delivering the paper, just as you, or rather your father who was driving, pulled out of the parking place.

YOU MIGHT THINK

You might think a bus ride would feel like any other transportational experience, isn't it so? A bit dirtier than an airplane, a bit less classy than the Metroliner, but taken all at a time. . . . Well, let me convince you — seeing's believing, so they told us in school. You see to the left the mist rising off the Hudson, the hills and rocks of deciduous New York to our right.

The mist stays with us to Connecticut. I have tried to attract you to conversation, offered you raisins and dried apples I packed this morning with my cheese sandwich, but hesitantly you accept, as though you fear more commitment than you could possibly handle, this Tuesday morning in July. You've been in the city six weeks, now you're returning to Hartford. You smile as you eat my raisins.

IN midsummer there was a roof of oak leaves along our
street. Even on those muggy Boston afternoons when
the air in the house was heavy and motionless, the street
outside was cool. Summer evenings softball teams
would play on the diamond just across the street from
our front porch. Sometimes I'd sit on the white fence
at the edge of the street and watch, but more often I'd
be right up against the wire mesh of the backstop – a
structure that rose swaying in the air, and though I'd
climbed part way up I didn't have the guts to climb over,
which I'd heard that Tom Farber, from down the street
and five years older, had done.

The softballs snapped from the pitcher's arm, a wind-
mill delivery, to the catcher's mitt barely ten feet from
me. Since there weren't any lights all the games had
to be played early: just right for me, kid that I was, I
could still be home by dark.

GOOD HARBOR

AS THE PLANE LEFT NEW YORK

As the plane left New York I whispered "good-bye, Papa," the tears rolling over my beard to fall on your tweed jacket, you know, the herringbone that fits me perfectly, the one I always used to borrow when I came to visit. At the service Leonid played a Bach partita. Cleo told Deb she had never heard him play so beautifully. Pablo's elegy (your intelligence, your curiosity, your humility) you would perhaps say 'shit' to, not that it wasn't true: but I have seen you cry, knew your pain and fear.

Last summer, do you remember? – your ashes scattered now to the ocean – we visited Ellis Island, where seventy years earlier your mother entered the country, her two-year-old daughter sick, also dying. . . . Congestive failure, arrhythmias: the words are flat, removed from your body warm in our last embrace (. . . your face reflected in my spoon).

The empty halls on the island whisper a confluence of ghosts and echoes. The plaster flakes and decays, the roof collapses. You can hardly climb the stairs, your muscles, your heart weak – "a gallant man," Bernie said. So much vigor and spirit and warmth and understanding still to give.

The old ferry lies rotting by the quay. Your sister is buried in the area closed to tourists, by the old hospital. It is summer and the trees are green, sway in the wind; the clouds are building darkness; it's beginning to rain. From the boat we can see the Jersey shore. The rain is flattening the water. The lightning streaks to the shore,

splits the clouds second by second. We sit and watch
the island receding behind us, trees green, red buildings
decaying. Rain is tumbling upon the water, the island,
the boat. Watching the island, we float in a steel boat
upon the harbor.

AT THIS MOMENT PERHAPS

FROM the windows a countryman of the fourteenth or fifteenth century would no doubt believe he was in hell: the gray skies, the lifeless vertical surfaces of flat rock, the glittering flickering panes, the rising trails of smoke. My wife is walking the dog, I am practicing the piano. On the balcony (a view of the river, the park) our tomato plants flourish. The notes of the piano stagger in my sudden thought. My wife is out walking the dog.

A countrywoman of the fourteenth or fifteenth century would no doubt believe she was in hell: flat surfaces, gray light, quick reflections, funnels of smoke. The morning paper lies next to the vitamins. At this moment perhaps my dog is taking a shit out in the street. Taxis puff in the sudden curse of notes from my window.

YOU COME IN THE ROOM

Mountains float a dark sky: this desert valley (*only* 98 they said today), last town on the highway – and yet a stream raises cottonwoods each side, corn shimmering in a hot wind.

You come in the room, the back of my head pressed against the pillow. You ask and I feel as though this day, this clarity of vision – a sheet to cover my belly, my knees: as though this brilliant clarity and weight of heat were conscious of my need. . . .

Smile this day upon us, clear heat of desert, touching us through curtains. What folly brings you here day upon day as though nothing has changed? Well, you say, these mountains don't they hasten tall and empty?

At three this morning I saw: eastward above dark mountains, Saturn glitter and wink.

THESE MAY WELL BE

I descended out of the coastal hills. It was a soft morning and fog lay upon the thick leaves of the town. Streets glistened with fog. The silence of the morning moved with it.

I found I would not trust myself to the ferry, that meager scrap of metal, upon the shifting inland sea. Waves rose green and shattered upon the breakwater. Hastening through the town I soon found myself in alluvial swamp, but now I cannot retrace my steps.

Fog muffles the turmoil of my passing, mud-sucked, branch-snapping. Wherever I step, I sink. Dead trees loom above me. I struggle through the silence, stumbling in the obstinate soaked earth.

THESE may well may be my last entries. Shortly I will reach the border – from there the map shows only a blank surface, white, featureless. In reality the mountains continue to the horizon, low ridges and isolated peaks dark against the sky: a pine-and-maple wilderness filled with the river. I have seen no one now for several weeks. I thought I saw a wolf one night (a silver shape running stiff-legged, faint in the moonlight) but the moon hadn't yet reached its second quarter. Perhaps it was imagination. I continue to have enough food.

My journey has taken me northward from the defunct cities, following the river or its tributaries (many dry now in the the dry summer), angling toward the border. The old north-south footpath traversed some of these ridges – in the midst of the bush I have found the going easy: the trees large enough to block under-growth, the ground clear and spongy with years of pine-needles, the forest dark and silent even in the middle of the day.

Today I came upon a curious scene. I had been walking for several hours in a sporadic thundershower, the sky remaining gray but little rain falling. The river is brown and sluggish here, scummed over in stagnant pools away from the main channel. I was walking slowly, looking for a spring where I could find some clean water, when I came upon an old bridge abutment rising gray and decayed out of the mud. Many of the stones had split and fallen, and the bank had collapsed so that it partly covered the base of the huge support. But there the thing stood.

Undergrowth near the bank had destroyed every trace of a road, but some twenty meters from the water I came upon asphalt. Imagine, asphalt! Night was just beginning to close down, with a luminosity that I think occurs only on these clouded summer evenings, just before dark. The air seemed to glow and the leaves of maple and fir flowed with darkness. The asphalt at times was nearly invisible, so many plants grew through it and obscured it; at times it stretched, a clear path, for many feet through the forest. Through leaves and branches I saw the trace of a white line – radiating, it seemed, into a twilight of dripping leaves.

VACATION

You go away for a short vacation back East, where the trees are big and the air this time of year has a delicate edge of selenium from the computer companies out along Route 128. It seems to you everyone is coming a little unstuck. You notice new buildings going up fifty or so miles from the center of Boston, squat concrete structures backed into hillsides. All of them face away from the city.

Your return flight is canceled in New York and you are given a ticket back in someone else's name. At the last minute they try to stop *him* from going on the plane after you. "I'm sorry, sir, but you can't go on that plane," you hear behind you – "you see, you've already boarded and we can't allow your ticket to be used twice."

Stranger still, when you get home. Someone else is living in your apartment; or rather someone else is living where your apartment would be if the building was where you left it just a couple of weeks ago. But there's another building at your address which clearly, what with all the detail around the eaves, is at least a hundred years old. And it isn't what it once was, it hasn't been painted for years. . . .

Fortunately they still recognize you at the bank – but everyone calls you Colonel and people you've never seen before seem to know who you are. "Good show there, Colonel," you hear one woman say to you, "I knew you had it in you." When you telephone, none of your friends are in, or their lines have been disconnected.

Wandering around in confusion you pass the Army Intelligence laboratory, and as you reach for the doorknob you are quite sure that you've come to the right place.

GARAGE

Iт's hard to tell, the picture's all scrunchy and smudged, but it seems like the dictionary defines my garage roof as a "hip" roof – that is, one where the slant changes, like a barn – so I suppose you could say that my garage, sitting back on the southwest corner of my lot, looks like a small barn with even smaller maples growing up all around it (no buds yet, though I've been looking), a lilac, and a couple of hydrangeas or snowball bushes we called them as kids.

Last week I went out there to close the southernmost of the two large doors, which, though its hinges are gone, was flapping in a high wind that brought a blizzard to most of the Midwest but fortunately no snow here. You'd best close that door before it gets ripped completely off those hinges, I heard a voice say. Behind the lawnmower disabled now by winter a pallet I'd left for some reason had fallen and was covered with straw. What's straw doing in the middle of the city? This is my story, kid. You think it's easy wintering here with a bit of straw and a pallet separating me from the concrete slab, a roof and some drafty walls. . . .

Right away I knew I'd made a mistake. What's an old man doing in my garage anyway? It would be easy to say it was just the door flapping in the wind, call it a winter breeze. Fortunately the neighborhood was empty. That's right, no one around, that's exactly how it was.

GOOD HARBOR

. . . one by one
The roses fall, the pale roses expire
Beneath the slow decadence of the sun.

— Ernest Dowson

WE'RE lying together, you and I, in a dark bedroom in a musty New York hotel. Our bed is opposite the windows, the blinds are drawn. Outside it's one of those cloudy December afternoons, but on the other side of the windows there's only a brick wall and the bottom of a roof. And so even if it were a bright, incredibly clear, incredibly blue afternoon, we wouldn't be able to see more than this trickle of gray light through the gray venetian blinds.

We lie in bed now, barely touching each other, as light and cold air seep in through the windows, warmth suffuses from the radiator clanking in the corner. We can hear the pigeons in the eaves of the roof opposite us.

I can't stand those pigeons, you say. They make me think of death.

I'm lying now with my head between your arm and your breast, smelling the warmth of your body, and I say

Think of love, that's what you make me think of. And I reach over then to stroke your belly and your thighs.

I love when you touch me, you say. Never stop touching me.

The sheets are musty—and the bed creaks in this

78

dark New York hotel room, while outside the pigeons moan in the eaves opposite our room.

* * *

But you always said that many things were possible, not least among them love, and though I wasn't fool enough to believe you, I always thought that at least you believed yourself.

Should I then say

So finally you've left me. And why, just when we seemed closest, when it seemed that summer would at last leave us alone to pursue the bright course of our existence?

I remember the spring. We held each other in the warm April darkness, on the damp hillside, while the clouds rushed above us. . . .

You are back now, I suppose, in the Midwest, in your house on the lake. And do you sit there, in the heavy sweet summer darkness, while your wife plays you Haydn? Do you sit there thinking fondly of the art you may produce from some vague memory of a winter's loneliness?

* * *

As Dylan said, country music stations play soft, distance tuning them out as we drive north, still winter here, snow on the ground. Finally there is silence and static, the last station from somewhere out of state fading entirely. We spend a final few minutes driving along dark roads in the beginning of a spring blizzard.

The hotel seems once to have been a saloon, with rooms above the bar. The owner, a Polish woman in her sixties, has a passion for plants. We exchange a few words in the hall. How do you mange to grow such plants all the way up here? Tropical growths a yard across sprout green in the drafty halls, the small rooms. An asparagus fern is the largest I've ever seen indoors, a rubber plant stretches across two windows, philodendra creep into corners and across ceilings. I tell her it's the love inside her and we smile at each other on my way to the well-furnished bedroom: a rocking chair with floor-standing ashtray, hand-woven carpet, a huge schefflera, and an uncurtained window looking out on Norway pine and a woodshed. Wagon tracks, white with snow, curve into the dark forest. Somewhere a dog barks, once, twice.

At night I'm with you in an island wilderness, a canyon a sluggish river flows through. Enormous birds are circling overhead.

*　　*　　*

You walk through Customs smiling and embrace me in the same moment you remove your pack. Hi kid. You take me home to your family's apartment looking out at the city from some immense height, seagulls gliding by the living-room windows.

The apartment is busy with a cocktail party. Feigning fatigue, you lead me to the guest room where we're served dinner by uniformed maids. After chicken cacciatore and wine you light a candle and we talk, looking out at the rainy night. We discuss your trip. You tell me, upon questioning, of your few brief affairs. Slowly we undress each other.

In the midst of this a maid enters. We believe she stands watching us a moment before she leaves.

*   *   *

There's a large park across the road and the water spreading blue and pristine in the afternoon. We walk across the salt-rusted bridge, the sun hot, lovers lying in the grass, dogs running in packs.

The boathouse is light and sandstone, windows twenty feet high. The windows are empty now in the afternoon sunlight. The earth breathes dry, dry, dry, this summer, the cedars dark and dry.

SNOW AT TEN O'CLOCK

LEAVING the house to walk the dog, I hear what sounds like kids arguing up the block. It's about three and that's when kids walk home from Thoreau and St. Bernard's Schools, still bundled up for winter. It's cloudy – a low ceiling, perhaps 100 feet; it's drizzling, drops blowing in the northwest wind. . . . Seems like soon it'll rain harder.

But no, it's not kids – low overhead, my god, it's geese! – an irregular V-formation, seems like right over the blue spruce, the geese squawking, arguing back and forth, complaining to each other. I think: geese, it's spring – though the lakes are still frozen. My dog and I walk down along the tracks, and I realize that these geese, they're flying south . . . . What? – southeast, to be precise. This morning I heard on the news: a storm moving in from the northwest. Rain here, north of here snow. Minneapolis, I heard, already has five inches of snow.

I imagine the geese, leaving Illinois early this morning (fog and pale cornstubble in a muddy field), running into snow and a thirty-knot wind coming right at them, as the aviators say, at ten o'clock. No wonder they're complaining. It's beginning to rain harder, my dog and I walk back along the tracks. The geese must have turned right around, now they're flying with the wind, flying low, looking for a place to spend the night. I think of the map: perhaps they're heading off toward the marsh at Lake Kegonsa (a straight shot southeast), where white snow and brown cattails surround the open water of Williams Creek.